Second Skin

Jeanne Marie de Moissac

Second Skin

For Suzanne,

A Kindred, a
Shining soul.

Great to
reconnect!

Best wishes
Jeanne-Marie

COTEAU BOOKS

Edited by Elizabeth Philips.
Cover and book design by Duncan Campbell.
Cover illustration by Bernice Friesen.
Printed and bound in Canada.

The publisher gratefully acknowledges the financial assistance of the Saskatchewan Arts Board, the Canada Council for the Arts, the Department of Canadian Heritage, and the City of Regina Arts Commission, for its publishing programme.

Coteau Books celebrates the 50th anniversary of the Saskatchewan Arts Board with this publication.

Canadian Cataloguing in Publication Data

De Moissac, Jeanne Marie, 1959
Second skin
ISBN 1-55050-142-9

1. Title.
PS8557.E48193S43 1998   C811'.54   C98-920113-9
PR9199.3.D434S43 1998

Coteau Books
401-2206 Dewdney Avenue
Regina, Saskatchewan
S4R 1H3

AVAILABLE IN THE U.S. FROM:

General Distribution Services
85 River Rock Road, Suite 202
Buffalo, New York,
USA, 14207

For my children, Jesse and Rachel

And in memory of Jerry Hindley
1951–1991

Contents

My Grandmother's Rosary

Stone Maiden

Warrior

My Grandmother's Rosary

Lamb Skin

I lay her on her back over a five-gallon pail
stood on its head the bottom becomes a table

and her neck drops back
so soft
tight dark curls
mama licked her dry
though she never took a breath

T cut on her chest
this jackknife is dull
or this hide is tougher
than it looks

Down the belly first
careful not to nick the gut
bit by bit
slice by slice
the wool
the skin
the skin

and when I've cut far enough
to get my fingers through
I work with both hands
one holds the knife
one works the skin
cut and push
cut and push
almost peels away

Undressed now
she is pink in my hands
looks sweet
woolly little face
four black feet
eyes won't close

I put her in the shit-pile
cover her with straw
hold her loose skin in my hands
outside baby soft
inside cool and smooth

You can come now I call
and my daughter comes in
through the barn door
she's been waiting
takes the skin
presses it against her face

Are you ready I ask
and she smiles
nods
hands me back the skin

slowly she undresses
neatly folds her clothes
lays them in the straw
stands before me
lifts her arms

and I wrap her
cover new breasts in woolly lamb skin
take the one I skinned before
stitch it to the fresh one
tiny stitches
neat and black
in and out I push my needle
tie the tails between her legs

There you are I say
as I secure the knot
How is that

and she moves
slightly bent
shoulders curving in

It feels so tight
and her eyes shine full
in the barn's dull light

Shush, my pretty girl
I whisper
Soon you'll forget
It fits so well
A second skin
Soon you'll forget

Heave Ho

goes the clothes basket
the week in my arms
past hips, over shoulders
all the way to the top of my head
shift wet weight, settle it there
the silver bands around my wrists
catch the early sun

my feet move in rhythm with my breasts
lift and sway
my spine's gone straight as an aspen's trunk
vertebrae stacked, discs in place
roots embedded in ancient waterways

lift and sway
it's safe to come up now
black mother of snakes
I've invited you

coil up inside this slender trunk
white strong centre round my blood core
then dark   this wood I've become

outside I've spun paper in wasp nest layers
one inside the other
and finally these lichens
you've painted gentle red
light dabs
proof of my devotion

lift and sway
my arm steadies the load
bracelets tinkle music
beautiful as the song of my breath

Clothes-line

the absurdity of laundry is the constant Mondays
one after the other like a line full of clothes-pins
cancan dancers holding blue jeans between their muscled legs

I'm there in season

the change coming as dryer lint piles high in the burning
        barrel
on that first fine Monday it disappears
a winter's worth of drying up in quick smoke

Monday, sure of its own regularity, sets the week's tone

will these clouds open and send another rinse cycle
can I stir enough wind to flap this wash
smoothly as the last
or will it hang still
wait for my iron

I fill these same three lines Monday after Monday
but the jeans have somehow grown longer
panties more generous
wedding towels frayed and washed thin

and are these my son's white socks or his father's
at the end of the day
I'll sort them by hole-size and shades of grey

my own clothes have faded
each wash draining a little more colour
but soft; they'll make rags as fine as my wedding towels

Soldiers, come in

come in from the line
you are frost-bitten grey as this early winter sky
too much snow too soon to continue
your sturdy devotion deserves a warm place to winter
come into my kitchen, sit by my fire

*

regardless of what they say, magpies
are hopping sure as anything right into the garage
for dog-food, dogs aren't moving
can't say I blame them with this November wind-chill

these mitts are too clumsy for clothes-pins
I pluck them bare-handed and drop them into the egg-pail
no brown and white pattern there
the hens aren't laying these days   *scratchings* – sometimes
the only thing left to talk about is the hens and the weather
"8 eggs – those clouds look like snow" – *scratchings*
anyways, no eggs today and either these clothes-pins
already grey as Grandfather's barn
want to winter out again or my fingers have lost feeling
down go my fingers after them into the new bank, snow
burning like a nipple clamp, moving into nerves
finding endings

*

I finally have you in my pail, old soldiers
out of order and at ease, winter is here
come in by my fire, red as my fingers

Scratchings

they don't come out to eat for five days
after two I take pity
put a lid full of water in their box
ten white pullets huddled in the dark
light coming in round holes
punched through the cardboard

the old hens cackle, stop in turn to peck the box
then getting bored with this game
chase meaty grasshoppers
sluggish in the autumn drizzle, and step three-point
scratch calligraphy in the cold mud
on both sides of the fence

my nephew from the city, almost three, comes to visit
I want to take him to the hens
but the flies on the deck humming full of sunshine scare
him to the dirt, the dirt on the ground muddy full of
spring scares him to the van and he won't come out
to see those boxed hens – only two left now
almost seven years since they came out
debeaked under-bite
never could catch grasshoppers

Tic Tac Toe

the water of this solstice carnation is stale as rotten teeth
stale as the air between them
their lips meeting
 only lips
  no other part of their bodies shall touch

  kiss of mother-in-law
so must this be it then, no contact, save children
when there goes the man-parade
somehow they all sniff her out
father said she should sit like a lady
but it never felt right to her
knees don't belong together

Come on then, she says to herself

they'd see what she really wanted
  a double take, kitty playing chase

who will be first
who is number two
tic tac toe
one says stop
the other says go
who gets the kitty
that's what I'd like to know

meantime she's found the pipe and sometimes she's the bowl
and sometimes she's the stem and sometimes she's both of them
but mostly when she sends away the smoke
the stale air clears oh, the sun comes slow this time of year

Switch

she sighs, opens her eyes

slip this around your shoulders, my mother tells me, holding a
blouse of silky green, *but first give me back that stick*

when I won't give it over, how could she believe I'd be ready
she covers my designs with the green
closing her eyes wasn't good enough, tries to take this thin
switch but these fingers won't loosen, they've grown around
the wood
this would be a new rule, mother, and I've
only just learned the rhythm of the other

besides, I've found beauty in the pause
my mind still enough to see the *W* on a blade of brome

besides, why else the thistle in my garden, not a weed
I'd choose, yet I know my life when I pick it bare-handed

besides, I see nowhere to fall when I look into your eyes mother

Olfa Knife

I press my finger to an olfa knife
sharp blade, machine shop dirty
it isn't deep but pours red out the end

I see your need
your cheeks drawn
whiskers dark on pale   you ask
I give   because I don't know how to say no
I try
curl my tongue against the roof of my mouth
form the round *O* with my lips
push it out quiet; you don't hear

Open up, then
I say
Before it clots

my finger scabs over, thick and dark
and when I can't leave it I pick it off
bit by bit

Look
I show you the new pink underneath
I am healed
and you smile that thirsty look

the knife is dull now
old blade, last blade and you help me push it in

and when I open
wider than before
deeper than the last time
you catch your drink

lapping lapping

I hold your head
stroke your hair
sing gentle murmurs in my throat

when you've finished
and you kiss my lips
I taste my salt

Fault-line

Mother thinned her cabbages, broccoli and cauliflower
then sent me the seedlings in a grocery-bag-lined
        cardboard box
careful of the bottom, slightly wet
it gives with the weight of its contents
I open the box in the garden
on top are the planting instructions
printed clearly on pink notes
and the dirt is black
I remember how it was slough-bottom sticky in the spring
how it clung to the soles of my feet
not so dense as the earth in my garden, but blacker
the mixing will do it

the wind picks up the pink notes, teases me into a chase

I plant my seedlings quickly before supper (there never really is
time to transplant) and none too soon, she dropped them off at
the John Deere Dealership first thing this morning – seems
there's lots of deer this year – mostly twins they say
        and when I call to thank my mother
for the cabbages, broccoli and cauliflower
(we do most of our business by phone)
she tells me my sister hit a deer on the Deer Foot
the closest some people get to wild life,
who knows what business she had there,
the doe I mean – perhaps it was an ancient trail
and she just for an instant forgot about the freeway, or do they
follow a fault-line, find their quiet trails
wind their quiet trails
and you shall see the circles where they've gathered to sleep
how dew gathers like a net, catching all the grasses
as doe-coloured lichens gather on the stones

I follow my own fault-line
moving from one seedling to another, making amends
at the end of it all is the cabbages, broccoli and cauliflower
and how the dark green leaves rescue me
like the flowers Gramma cut every morning
must have rescued her from the deep crack
as the fault-line swells and recedes

Tapestry

one thing you can save is hair
snip snap go my scissors
my mother watches while I sweep around the stool
"You'll want to save that dustpanful," she says
as I scoop it up
an inside story of a long Sunday visit
where she sat quiet with her hands
while her father and his friend
changed the world in the parlour
while their wives exchanged recipes
and niceties in the kitchen

how there was a picture in the room where she sat
a tapestry of hair: coiled vines and flowers in full bloom
muted in shades of greys and white, browns tightly woven
bits of auburn for accent to centre a single golden rose
a garden under plated glass

I wonder how many dustpanfuls I'd have by now
enough, I imagine for a prairie winter scene
she's been grey for some time now
something to see, something for my wall
but even defined in a frame, still not as real
as minutes stretching across time
like hands held in mine
my daughter's, my mother's
connecting me, one world to the other

The Mrs.

her house, at the bottom of a long hill
is entombed in caraganas and a mirage of dark spruce

I push open the front door and walk into the parlour
a chair decomposing in the corner, waiting for company
tongue & groove floor, gravelled
with many generation of pigeons
what would she say if she saw
or is that her now, broom in hand
sweeping the dust away twice a day
that blows in from the broken prairie on the east wind
through the kitchen, oven door hanging wide
loaves set to cool

it rustles the wallpaper, that east wind
pattern on pattern, each layer of her life hanging in strips

what was her name? I ask the farmer who stops seeding to
interrupt my nosiness with his own

John's wife? now that I can't recall
we just called her the Mrs.
wouldn't speak a word of English – that much I remember
kept mostly to herself

and where might your garden be, Mrs.?
I find it so close – the whole prairie
yet she used space like a city woman

the prairie has crept back, filtered through the caraganas
her first spears of asparagus are reaching through the fescue
and the rhubarb, tender dark greens
competes with a wild rose bush and buffalo sage

Sod

the willows my grandmother planted have
grown their life into the prairie
and are dying, trailing grey bones
across the path to her first house, blocks of sod
one piled on the other
held fast with the deep roots of prairie wool

I see her washtub and butter churn
milk pails by the door
a basin chipped and well worn
that held rising bread
brought in vegetables and carried out chicken slops

all her work
all her babies

year after pregnant year
mostly coming too quick
dying before they filled their lungs
tucked lovingly into the cold prairie

I'm sure she plugged herself with rags
milked the next morning
kept so busy there was no time to think
leaving a legacy of hard work, prayers
and the willow's grey bones

Church Dress

I pull a dress over my head
too fancy really for the garden
but what's wrong with being a princess
besides, I'm loose and cool underneath

rain the night before
the dirt on the soles of my feet alive
and giving sweetly with my weight
my hands find rhythm in the weeding
out they come
out they come
and I see my grandmother, bent over in her garden
old church dress loose, dull black against bright poppies
hiked high at the back, the tops of her rolled-down-nylons
end exactly above her white knees
and the weight of the rosary, coiled in her pocket
shifts the hem of her dress slightly right

I finish, too hot to work long
scrub the earth from my hands
splash my sun-stained face
and when I peer in the mirror
hanging over the sink
she is there

Jane Siberry brings it out of me

This is the darkest time, Grandmother
when roosters crow in the sun at two
the howling wind, wailing, bead-counting
little girl with her boots full of slough
crying time
scrying time

Sh she dream-whispers to me *No, cheri*
Careful who you call
wait for da swell of da crescent to appear
protection now would cost too dearly

But I need you now, your webbed hands under my chin
as I spin my life

And I'll crawl into this shadow and call
Grandmother
here I am
won't you send me on the sash of your mass-black silk
one of them sucky cheek kisses
I've tried to pass them round as best I can, but lately
I've run a little short

And would you lend me your rosary
to spin through my fingers
as I wait out this shadow moon

Duet

for the sisters

they come together
these two as halves of apples, cut neatly
starred core pentacled with seeds

they come together along the bench
their hands almost identical
against the flats and sharps
and me the audience of one

Eve plays the melody
hands white, smooth as ivory
and small, the size of my son's
yet the strength is there in the fingertips
taut skin now her hands have grown in

Aimée is harmony
fingertips light and sure
nails cut quick and short
and knuckles red with mothering
veins slightly raised, not ropy
too soon for that – yet the skin is looser
as if the hand inside has shrunk
like mom's, like mine

and I look down at them folded in my lap
remember the game we used to play at the table
while we ate our apples
called pile of hands
the bottom slapping the top
quicker now and quicker
until our hands blur one into the other
all into our mother's hands

Beacons

loose wet snow fell in the dead calm
before the blizzard sent it into a white-out
blew topsoil from under the snow
right into the house
flash frozen on the door
and I prayed if this great mother of a prairie
was going to exfoliate, let my children be gathered
around the wood stove, woman's black belly
heating up the house, and if I had my grandmother's rosary
I'd have spun that one in my hands to Sweet Mary
like my sister who tells me on the phone her man put his head
out the window to see the yellow line
my other sister might have to wean that baby quick
if she can't get home from work

mom phones, tells me how Grandad was caught in a blizzard
in the middle of White Shore Lake, how he gave his team
their heads and how Gramma
sent the hired man up the windmill
to hang a lantern in the blizzard, a beacon like my candle
in the window and I don't see them drive up
they just appear out of the white

My Grandmother's Rosary
for Jesse

you see the reaper
first thing on the way out
and you open your mouth
cry that you're doing it again
cry at the sight of her bones
bones of the grandmother you never knew
grandmother of the other side

after your first breath
she tells you the secret your mother can't whisper
the truth about these times
then, the introduction to the angels
who really need none, they're in it for the long haul
but the reaper is also the teacher of manners
the common denominator

which grandmother pulled my daughter out of me
I wonder that
and what would my father's mother have done with her rosary
crystal beads, seeds of prayers
buried with her, binding her wrists
finger bones clacking like knitting needles
as she counts out her prayers

would my mother's mother, small hands
seized together in a claw
have been capable
all the kisses in the world
wouldn't open those fingers

I suppose any grandmother (there are many grandmothers)
would do – though our name honours the father
the waters where we swam were waters of the mother
waters of the daughter

23

released by the sharp nail tip of one long finger
as grandmother reaches in
   at birth this veil is thin
   at birth the veil is broken
when she pulls it aside you see her bony face
   cry at the death of it
   cry at the life of it
and she puts you in the arms
of your first lover, o blessed mother

Stone Maiden

Tail lights

one of those late trips, shopped out
mind on overload, home from the city
the truck is quiet while we watch the wind
skim long fingers of snow across the highway
and the oncoming headlights send their beams up
like beacons into the night

we're tailing this van, you know the type
just like an asshole everyone's got one
and there's too much traffic to pass

when he says what do you think those tail lights
look like on the back of that van

so we all look
a devil pops in my head
but I say nothing, sure that somene else
will see his red horns and slanted eyes

2 dolphins, says Rachel, jumping out of the water
at the same time
and my devil's horns leap
eyes turn to breaking water

I doubt it, says Jesse, it's a crab
don't you get it, see the pincers
and graceful dolphins turn into
the snappers of a sideways bottom scuttler

your turn, dad

he'll say a devil
how could he not see it

a well, he says, deep and full of water
and the lights at the top are covers
see? an open well
no, only now I don't want to say how I see tails, horns
billy-goat-beards on pointed chins, long muscles
cloven hooves and narrow erections
in more than tail lights

but they're waiting

I blurt it
in the silence I wonder what kind of mother I must be

what's a devil? asks my daughter

Rear-View Mirror

Darkness, nothing but darkness beyond
my headlights. I speed, my lights embrace the white
the winter – and I'm lulled
into complacency by the heater's hum
warm wind on my face, the CBC discussing
something profound

although I'm not really listening, instead pondering
life's simplicity, my go-cup nestled in its holder
filled with fresh 7-11 coffee. I open my window
a crack, flick out my cigarette, watch in the rear-
view mirror as it explodes on the frozen highway
a careful sip – sweet brew on this cold dark night

and I catch something on the radio. Something about
aborting female foetuses. I click it off, spill hot
coffee on my jeans, feel it spread
turning cold. I light another cigarette.

The Ex

Even though the truck is parked close
it seems a different space outside the noise of the rides.
We've left the midway, full of being amused,
and not up for the energy raised for the night
we buckle ourselves in.
"A moth!" Rachel freezes,
she who helps her father pile dead sheep
in the front-end loader. The moth, trapped inside a sweater,
throws herself again and again against the window pane.
"Get it away!" cries Jesse,
he who captures double agents
and details his gopher kills over supper.
"It's just a little moth," says their Dad,
"what's the big deal?"
"I know," says Jesse, "it's too weird."
"They're ugly," says Rachel, clear as that.

I flick on the interior light, catch the wings
in my fingers. I am not afraid like I used to be.

We'd chase around the table if one got in the kitchen
scream until Mom crushed it in a kleenex, spilling the dusty
shadow. It would have been the extreme torture, horrible as
kissing the toilet plunger – tied in a chair in a darkened room
mouth forced open, small bright light
fixed in the centre of your tongue
and the room would be filled with dusty millers
dark ashes in your mouth.

I don't know when I stopped being afraid of shadows,
perhaps when I found a place for the darkness
perhaps when I understood the pull of the light.
I open the window wide, release my catch into the night.
She flies towards the midway
to perish in an ecstasy of light.

Lady of the Flies

winter is coming
that instant when nothing is the same
that instant when the flies go to sleep
and as they bring the warm
they take it with them when they go
people are chatting now about the signs
the light, the gossip of the geese
the snow geese banked against the south side of the hill, see
how they will prepare the green to give way to the white, see
how they cool the earth with the flap and fan of their snowy
snowy wings

meanwhile, I'm the Lady of the Flies
they've moved from the slaughterhouse
my kitchen has become,
gathered in my truck, and I watch while they fuck
in the sunshine on my visor o I've opened my window
driving down the highway tried to brush them out
I even left it open at the abattoir in Vanscoy
you'd think that would be a tempting spot for flies
    John used to own it – he told me once how long it took
        to stop
  a steer's beating heart, how tightly he had to squeeze
I've shut this party down, invited them to leave the most
polite way I know how, seems to me they fly back in the truck
at a hundred kliks – quickest fix is to smack them, but
there's enough of that already – the newest rage for little girls
is called Lip Smackers, Rachel collects them all

the latest rage came upon my children when I brought
them home new mattresses, another change
blame me, blame the mother the whole day through
the whole way through
my son swears he'll shred it with his jackknife
my daughter flies at me with her small hard fists
while her water-bed drains away

I only wish the phone line would die
I only wish the stone maiden would save me

she's the one to clear the way for messages
travelling down from light
growing like squash starts seed small
green leaf draining life from the seed
length of vine pulling itself from the leaf
fruit drawing its heaviness from the vine
until giddy with abundance, it bursts

how if you don't let the messages come they settle like tears
you keep in your eyes, how they would be sour
how they would burn like a gilt in heat, dink in another pen

desire – where body and mind find common ground, sacred
            space
look, you say, but my vision is restricted
not like my entourage of flies who follow me in a cloud
changing my vibration
teaching me to see the periphery
I open more than my eyes in love
is there safety in the eyes of desire?
 o, service then is ecstasy

Velocity
for Daisy

i.

as yet unborn, still the tiger has stolen
whole lines of poems
stalked the dreams of young women and here am I
holding my tiger eye, my thumb rubs its smooth domestication
the light between the strati must surely hold all secrets

I'm caught up with the stone, with its manipulation
of my breath, caught up with the yellow, green and brown
the Christmas was brown – we didn't know how to act
we're used to putting on a tough-it-out face, a winter front

is all the water gone, then
cried away for our princess, the lovely Diana

I will take this tiger eye
wrap it with my hair
bind it in a prayer and send it off to Wales

send it off to Hilary, crying on New Year's Eve
candles burning everywhere
careful of your unbound hair
candles burning like all the screaming faggots
all the witches
all the cats

careful of the rats

ii

I seal this stone, this poem with a kiss
off to town I go, I can't stand not doing anything
and I can't leave the milk cow
    and I must thank thee for the milk cow
who really is as excessive as Christmas

Boxing Day night I find her out and into the barley
how she propels it out with such a fierce velocity
passion in motion, grace in suspension – like bubbles
trapped between the layers of ice
like tears inside masks – masks as dark as an old moon
on a Christmas when the snows never came

one can never be sure of the outcome
besides some days the milk cow
still kicks her pail over (no sense crying)
baptizes her wooden stall   *heartwood is stronger*
than sapwood, energy moving from inside out

if only I knew what the fuss was about
we all expected her to die sooner or later
even a real princess couldn't stand that much love
and speaking of excess, will the land-fills
look like an owl's pellet of nail clippings
plastic diapers and old cars
tiny foreskins and broken jars
layered like the stripes of my tiger eye?
will seven generations pass before the prairie claims
the land-fills, turns them into stone?

iii

stones are the bones stored in the grandmother
recycled like hand-me-down skates on clear ice in the coulee
bubbles between the layers
grace in suspension
the Cree say spirits move through the mist
passion in motion and it comes upon me so slowly
I don't realize until I drive inside

water without body
whispers through the coulees
inside it my gallant 4X4 speeds to town with this small stone
the mail
the mail
and I see only what is just ahead
just behind
just enough

Arc

the welder arcs blue into the night
through the window in the shop where he works late
and me on the deck with the last cigarette
my knitting tucked away until morning

my eyes are shut, still the light flashes behind my lids
and turns into Daddy's welder

we scatter
hide our eyes with his warning behind the shed
then creep up unobserved, his grey helmeted gaze
blind to everything but the two pieces he burns together

slowly, closer
a whole yarn ball of girls
see who will be first to stitch him in
that blue light some forbidden love

I pull my eyes back into this moonless night
flick my butt into what's left of winter
time for bed
I can't wait up while he welds the farm together

Cornflakes

for breakfast, no time to wash the porridge pot
Mom in her summer-suit irons white cotton blouses
in the middle of the kitchen

Mom he calls *what should I wear*
and she yells it upstairs as the starch dries in white puffs
he comes down, a perfect crease in his pants
and shaves to his reflection inside the cupboard door

our clothes are laid out on the counter and we dress
while she washes breakfast off the table
four little white panties flippy bright skirts blouses still warm
socks and polished shoes the night before
the last things are the hats she pins in our cropped hair
too short for secrets
and the white gloves she pulls on our brown hands

Mom always last to the car
red kisses on kleenex

"one of these days these boots
are gonna walk all over you" we sing
Sunday "Best by Request" twenty minutes to town
we fill the same pew and kneel, short martyrs on shiny wood
my sisters sing the high notes
I pretend, wait for the priest
like a bride he walks down the aisle, full of Christ

by the gospel I can't sit still
Latin doesn't move me and Mom pulls off her gloves
I put them on and they are white puppets
then angels with thin wings
I fly them till I get that look but the priest drones on
I slide to the floor
under the pew I am in a jungle of nylons and black leather

he pulls me up so quiet
I think he must want me on his lap
but no
out we go
up the aisle
and up comes sour milk and cornflakes

Dust Devils

born in blackened fallow
spinning they pick up Russian thistles
hitch-hikers down this summer road

she beckons and they come towards her
dusty circles round her bare feet
up her legs, round her waist
circle
    circle
        raised arms she sends them off

don't be late for supper, dear
mother calls after her
almost an afterthought
almost lost in the strawberries and heat

a mile down the summer road to the church
she doesn't stop to splash in the slough
or follow the duck limping away from her nest

grey wood shows through under white paint
long since peeled in the elements
front door groans open and the air inside
dense as the pigeon shit covering the eyes of Christ
nailed on solid oak
rushes out, pulls her in

the dust hangs in thick streams of sunlight
filtering through cracked stained glass
quiet, still enough to hear the ghosts of hymns
sung every Sunday, winter and summer
weddings and funerals of all those dead babies
lying unmarked in the church yard cemetery

when she's ready she walks the short aisle
genuflects low before the crucifix, the altar
slips into the confessional
unfolds the vestments neatly placed on the bench
as if the congregation was coming back

dressed in hallowed garb she ascends the altar
Dona Nobis Pacem Pacem Dona Nobis Pacem

after it is over
after raising her arms in final blessing
after changing into a little girl again
she leaves the church, late for supper
and stops by the slough to cool
the hot arches of her dusty bare feet

Birthing the goddess

she waits, small there
curled tight, feet in communion
with her face, so dark in my labyrinth
so still

finally she unfolds
pushes through
crowning light pours into the top of her head
fills her, plugs her in

I bear down
pressure on her forehead
that moment before I give way
I see her face between my legs
I didn't expect her to be so beautiful
I didn't need to be so afraid

once more, out she slides
and I pull her onto the softness of my belly
offer sweets from my breast

this journey towards light has ended
yet her eyes are shut tight with birth
she only sees into herself
I wipe them open with my hair

Pica

those first weeks
the time of turning leaves and flocking crows
she'd wake before the sun chased the dark away
and lie there craving what she didn't know
only the echo of some great need

then after the quickening
when her heart-shaped womb blood-stretched
rounded into a soft nest
she'd wake in the middle of the night
sit on the basement steps
and pull the dirt smell in through her pores

a potato, she pleaded on the coldest day
is what I need the most
and her man begged a pailful from the neighbour's root cellar
but when he put them in the sink she cried
No I want them as they are
and she sank her strong teeth in
found white flesh beneath the dirt and skin

and when this one she delivered
to the red-haired father's arms
he touched the dark hair with his calloused fingertips
wondering at her black-as-crow-feather eyes

Mermaids
   for Brody

he picks wild flax with its gentle scent
holds it in his small brown hand
tells me of the tiny spaceships
that fly out of his mouth
when he spits on the ground
I like to spit, he says
we're looking for a sheep to touch
and he plucks bits of wool from the buckbrush
binds his flax bouquet

o look the ocean he cries from the hilltop
when he sees the alkali lake, rain sign red
how can it be pink
and he dances on the gathering of stones
jumps from one to the other
  clouds are white
  sky is blue
  grass is green
can we go to that ocean, auntie
I bet the mermaids live in there

they'd have to be black ones to live in there, little boy
obsidian shining and smooth to their tail-tips
except their hair
white ropes dangling round them
ropes of crystal in the sun
except their garnet mouths

he finds a soft piece of wood to throw in for the mermaids
and the sun shines on the water
we walk through the mire
o see the thread-thin creatures
red faeries with salty wings
to shiver them through the water

o look a little worm a mermaid worm
they'll take the wood to the mermaids

so I clean us both up
black mud between our toes
and thank goodness he's still light enough
to swish around in the water

I set him on a rock to dry, with his flax bouquet
o auntie look – they're dead, he cries
their tiny heads droop sadly in his hand

we'll put them in some water as soon as we get back
the sun is hot, honey – they'll be fine
and I watch while the skin on his legs
washed by the brine
turns as white as salt

Sage

blood flowing down
I don't stop it up
instead I run until I lose the wind
            until the grasses only rustle
with the moving of my feet

there you are
like I always hoped you would be
  to pull me down beside you
hold my belly, swollen in your hands
press sage, pale green sponge between my legs

I will be your sister you whisper
as you unplait my hair
your fingers small butterflies
My eyes are open you say
All you see there is all I am

and you stroke my hair into the wind

When you are ready
I'll be your lover
my body stiffens, a quick inhale
Only when you're ready

I'll kiss you open
egg-smooth and open
fall into your moonless night
touch your spinning centre
hot and pulling in
open and letting go

you kiss my tear-swollen lips

And your mother
I will be your mother
I see you have need for one
    there   there
Fall quiet in these strong arms
I'll hold you safe against my breast
wait while love untangles you

my head drops into your lap
and when you draw away the sage
the prairie pulls the blood from me
fills her own cup with the blood from me
    I sleep
        I sleep

The gathering

one of the stones is flat
rusted with lichens
roots growing deep into the hill
into the prairie wool

I invite myself into the circle
and sit on this stone, my bones fit perfect
in a worn groove rocked there by many bones
many babies, while she tended fires
while she watched the sun dance the sky

I have walked this hill a hundred times
never saw the gathering of stones
never looked
never knew anyone had ever lived that close
and had to move

Stone maiden

"Shsh," says the stone maiden under my pillow
"Quiet your sounds and you'll hear
my breath on the tail-end of the North wind."

how intimate we have been with each other's curves
   see the chert curve of her cheek-bone
chiselled by time and the elements?

when I hold her, the thunder of the buffalo
rests in the cup of my palm

the swans took their turn to cast the spell
spinning autumn into winter
they haven't blown their trumpets here for seven seasons
and I haven't any reason why they stayed away so long
perhaps I'm only a rotation
I imagine they'd want a different
scene, fresh secrets, a new routine

and though the secrets aren't buried deep
they seem asleep just the same (it's all in a name)
asleep in the movement
the buffalo moved in great detail
grazed in rotation
the prairie giving forth in perfect order

the thunder of the hooves is still stored in the prairie
stored in the stone maiden's night-blue hair
it gathers in the hills
gathers on the plain and the buffalo run
towards the smell of rain that gathers in the woods
where wetness is hidden

and the thunder gathers in my feet
I take it in to town, dance it out at Bud's
to the blues' bass beat and Elsie asks me why I wanna be
a fucking Indian, and what the hell am I doing
with skins on my feet

she doesn't get the connection
or understand about the breath of the stone
and she won't let me touch her brown, angry cheek
her black eyes cooled only by the heavy blue line
she's drawn around them

The risk of frost

is clear, hard enough to kill the life
started too late with the rains
Rachel, hurrying the pumpkins in
leaves only touched with bran-frost
the gathering
          potatoes in the wheelbarrow
  green tomatoes in pails
and stones moving from earth to hand, hand to hand
gathering by the boxful in sunny verandas, on window sills
like the one my daughter found
at her Great Sand Hill
garnet shining out of granite
like beads of blood on alkali, quartz is salt-white and granite
mud a dark night

stones slip into conversations
and gather into circles like patterns in the wheat still standing
and the farmers hope the frost is hard enough
to turn the season quickly, easily as a woman changes names
but then they're always wishing for something
rain when there's sun
wind when there's none
sun when it rains well you get my point
my basinite point
stone-hammered smooth, cool as corn-silk —
Geronimo, do you feel the change coming
I see it set in an urgent line on Rachel's face
as the cold moves in
we can't cover everything
do you feel the change coming
stones don't feel it like pumpkins
they will gather under the snow, a bridge
to teach us our lineage
oh yes
and then we'll gather like geese
who follow home the moon and mother's milk

portulaca, midsummer's network of arteries
sprouts small leaves from the capillaries
as if nicked with a sharp paring knife

shallow roots come away easily, the earth damp with rain
that came too late for everything but the garden
don't think I don't feel remorse; anything that perseveres
in this heat deserves more than a noon-hour pull
quickest way to kill, heat of mid-day

only way to move the body is slowly
cat-stretch slowly – sometimes it's hard to tend everything
seasons changing with no reprieve
o if only Hilary's garden angel would grant me the will
to run naked through the corn

    – a tunnel so thick I can't see out the other side –
and taller than me, taller than me with my arms straight up
I'd feel my body in slow motion, voluptuous as fruit
giving way to the syrup
    tunnel deep as his eyes
Geronimo o how you looked at me
your eyes so black
no light to see
Agasi, he says
then disappears from my dream
wait, I say, I don't understand
what is expected of me

then I remember Emily from Red Pheasant
I met her up at Maymont
her and Little Leroy

Emily – are our arms long enough to bridge this abyss
you trusted me to swim over my head, you on my back
your small hands around my neck – don't let go
                    yet don't squeeze
                    so tight I can't breathe
                    you are safe in the comfort
                    of my body in this water

and I run through this tunnel of corn
a tunnel black as Emily's wet hair
clinging to her brown, brown, back
sweet second skin
and I know there is an end
after all I planted the row
and even though I can't see the light
I know it will be as bright as this noon-day
sun on just pulled weeds, mercy's kill

Agasi – a Cree word meaning "it is finished"

Berries

my feet find the deer trail
and the rest of me follows in perfect surrender
like going to bed with purple fingers
so many berries, all ripe at once
like giving in to the mantra of mosquitoes
chanting chanting
each OM a slightly different tone

the blood letting: a little here a little there and we see what
we end up with, never quite enough to go around when the dues
come in

and I do believe the saskatoons are best picked in the morning
still plump with the dew
and I do believe the saskatoons are best when the year
is deep-fried canola dry, only a few with blight
lichen-coloured, growing towards the sun

they offer cool respite; my fingers find the rhythm of the
picking, my fingers find the breath until the sun disappears
baby birds calling in their parents
there's more to it than just the feeding

*

the berries are black by moonlight
I'll be back tomorrow with more pails, more hands
get an early start
then I find the trail
what else to do but follow
and participate in an orgy of picking and eating
the biggest, the ripest – my pail is full
I can afford to be choosy

I come across her bed of flattened grasses already made
I see where she's laid her head
I see where she's tucked in her little one

suddenly I am right for the picking
ripe for the season
my feet planted in the sand
and the minute is removed

Tattoo

between the spinach and the garlic I've come clean
my clothes tangled in the squash

this wind is strong enough to blow the spinach pollen
into a fine yellow storm to dust my bare feet
they sink sweetly into the rain-softened dirt

my mind rests in the movement of my fingers
lulled by the rhythm of the weeding I let it wander
like this wasp I catch between my belly and my thigh
and before I can straighten
open this trap I've set with my body
she has put her stinger in

when I free her she flies wobbly at first
dazed at the sudden July sun
dazed at the sudden freedom

she finds her balance and sets her wings into the wind
the tattoo she leaves me turns red and white and red
like the peony blooms I'm drying
between the plastic grocery bags and Rachel's
red dress, turning them into winter roses

Warrior

Layers

This time she stands outside herself
looking at red buttocks
as he invites his friends in, the biggest first
he scoops a palmful of oil to ease the way
the woman lies prone on a rough bench
surrounded by erect flesh

she opens her eyes to surrender in her lover's face
as he sprays his milk upon her belly

they begin again

This time she's inside herself
                inside a curtained bed
transparent wings of gauze
layered red on white on red
parted over each pale breast
suckled nipples pink as Batoche new potatoes
she spreads her legs with a slow inhale
parted centre open open

in they come
one two three
and the father lies between her legs
the son at her breast, her mouth
and a tiny spirit buzzes in
between

she's outside the scene
she's spun below

This time she'll bring it in with her own quick hand
let the pictures come behind her lids
layered red and white and red
until all becomes earth

breathe me in, she calls to the skies
and she opens herself to the wind
fill me now, she calls to the sun
and he's caught between her thighs

Poached

his hands are quick
sure of their next move
and I watch him fill the saucepan half-full
a little butter, a sprinkle of salt
while it boils he cuts bread for the toaster

and picks his eggs from the basket
he prefers the pullets'
they usually hold together

then one by one he cracks them in a small bowl
slips them in the water
and it bubbles up around
white hugging yolk
yolk holding rooster dot
on a thin spiral

once in a while they fly apart
whites turn frothy like foam
on a sour slough
yolk a hard greenish orb
and tiny clot a red bindhi
floating to the top

Hooked

You have me hooked
right through the fleshy part of my cheek
as you pull me slowly in
gently in
so I'll think I'm not caught at all

You watched me in my watery world
that other place
silver and swimming
how you wanted me in your hands
and how I teased you

I never thought you'd find the right bait

how shiny
shiny and moving
how absolutely I need to bite
how perfect the pain of the hook slipping through

and when I'm finally caught
floundering between your small fine hands
how surprised you are to learn
I can't breathe
and out of my element
I'm not what you thought

Hag's Tit

the night Venus follows the crescent down, hag's tit in the sky
is long past, the thaw has awakened the benevolence of the soil
warm enough
wet enough to gather in my hands
I work, add winter-bleached grasses for strength

as I mold her head I find her face with my thumbs
what's this?
a beak?
and these bird eyes see all the way in, all the way out
        I find with my palms her hips
open them broad enough to birth the world
        I find with my fingers her nipples
pull them long enough to feed the world

and where might I find your arms, mother, your hands
holding yourself open as you sit atop Polaris
I reach in with two strong fingers, hollow out a dark space
that is only love, no teeth

you're the old woman who never dies
only changes into herself

Warrior

here you come again and I can't believe my luck
with your white stallion, barely restrained
prancing round my half-naked form

shall I let you pull me up behind you
push my nose in that place between your shoulders
sweet man-scent mixed with hay and horse sweat
safe, and I feel the rise and fall of you against my breasts

or would you hold me in the front of you
I would arch my back against your chest
my neck invites your lips
your free hand free and slow in my curves

how long would the moment be suspended in your
embrace
how long before you bid me change my shape

instead I tease you off your stallion
ask a solitary ride
you help me up and I kiss you full on your mouth
settle myself on his strong, white back

he becomes black and female

you watch, amazed at this turn
but surely you see how it is
how I've turned warrior after all this time

though it grieves me to leave you
with the part of me you will always have
there's no turning back

open your mouth as I leave
grit the dust between your teeth

if you need to find me
follow the thin trail of mare's milk
I will be waiting

Tufts

sometimes I wonder if I should ever leave the house
ever drive to town to walk up and down main street
and it doesn't matter if I screen myself with my kids

perhaps I need dark glasses to hide my wondering eyes
is that penis long and tapered at the end, is the base thick
is this one thick all the way, does it hide inside a foreskin
or has the end been cut away, a flower in perpetual bloom

hide my eyes from hands, some small enough to fit all the way
inside or great sausage fingers that would disappear
in the fleshy part of my hips, pulling them in, an anchor
and o those fingers would be long enough to find my
        little stone
my little bone

maybe if I cut my hair, or kept it tightly bound
long loose strands seem an open-ended invitation

or should I find those panties, long since tucked away
perhaps they sense she's bare she's bare in the way I walk

instead I lift my arms, ever so slightly
release the scent that collects in the small tufts of hair
see them trip on their wet tongues

X

I call her out to play and she comes, never shy anymore
from where I keep her, hiding underneath my sleep
she grows too big for the recess of my belly
uncurls her spine and each vertebra
as if stroked by a sweet lover
releases into itself

In one long movement she lifts her hair and stretches
her arms and legs an X, breathes deep, pulls it down
holds it, holds it
and as she pushes out the breath
the drums pound up her throat
low beat, coyotes' feet on hard-packed drifts of snow

*

After she is spent with the dance of herself
I send her home *Down you go* I say

lately, I fear
she comes unbidden, unleashed
her passage marked by the moist
tapestry between my legs

Cracks

sun bakes hot
splits the earth wide enough to push through
i test the air with my tongue
you stifle the impulse
to grind my head under your steel-toed boot

i take my chance in your confusion
shift my shape
desire clouds your reason
wait
one breath
two breaths

and then i slide across your belly
ride across your belly
flick my tongue into your ear
forked quick i lick
then graze down your cheek
leaving tiny marks of teeth
        prick
            prick
my legs wrap you
feel the texture of my weave
want a taste
sweet as earth
wet as spring

you shall enter
slip between the folds of my skin
feel me shudder
and you spill

after I will leave
slide away transformed
return to the ground
and you shall eat the skin that trails behind

Soot

she tends the fire before dawn with her breath
and rearranges half-baked logs in the night's ashes
rolls them on charred backs with quick fingers

they come away with the soot, meconium greasy
dark as his drooping wing
its shadow falling to the right
a shadow cast without the light
twisted wings, a weave of arms and wings
tips knotted square around the ash tree's lowest branch

she sees him, in the space where flame gives way to the smoke
knows him, yet the last time her nipples were two small stones

how full his lips that caught her kisses
gentle at first so she'd not send him back
his chest and back covered with a fine black film
long fingers that touched her open, pushed her open

now his crescent horns are tarnished
dreadlocks provide the backdrop
his back has become one with the tree
the bark, the skin
and his sharp hooves break water
spring water pulls the curls on his calves straight
reflects the erection that rests on his belly
one perfect tear clings to the winking-eye

she moves in to free him
she has to, it is time

she leans in close, close enough for him
to catch her sweetness on his tongue
her sweetness turns into his strength, his hope

she sets to work

a knot as tight as this should be difficult to undo
yet her fingers are quick, as if she tied the trick

when she releases him
separates wings from arms
his wings droop sadly behind him
his arms won't move until
she takes them in her strong hands
rubs the blood back in
and when he can lower them, finally
he touches himself, tastes himself
she defines him with her ahs and oohs
clearly as if she'd taken one sooty finger
outlined his form

he preens his dark wings
they catch rainbows from the fire's light
then she tends him with her breath, gives him back his shadow
the temperature drops as the sun comes up
the house cracks

Great Divide

I cross the divide where mountains free fall to prairie

cloud curtains open and snow-filled stubble reflects the sun
turns the hair on his arm to red-gold

kids play house with blankets
make smelly marker blueprints in the back seat

I move close buckle the middle seat belt
nudge him to find my nipple through two layers

Rachel leans over the seat *Daddy's gotta kitty cat*

and I purr
sleep against his leg
dream rough tongues and saucers of milk

Winter Nests

Cold, wet
days grow short
fall hangs near
the rams are fat
bored in their summer pen

I hear them from the clothes line
sheets slapping wet wings against my face
watch them back away
slowly
slowly
never losing eye contact
then run hard
throwing bulk and muscle into their heads
and I feel the dull thud between my eyes

time to open the gate

they leave their pen
heads split
scabbed over
to burst again
when tempers flare

and I smell them as they run past
through the open gate
they know exactly where they're going
no need to use the dog
musky hay and heavy
wish someone wanted me as much

ewes smell them too
fight for first place
first taste
swollen vulvas pink
they squat and pee their scent

rams' eyes glaze in smoky film
the first seed spills on the ground
they run from one to the other to the other
where to look
where to sniff
upper lips curled back
breathing ambrosia

Skirts

after two weeks with a pitchfork
my hands have changed shape
filled in, their backs bruised
by cramped quarters and contractions

*

I hear sheep are really stupid, says my friend from the city
as I coax him to the barn, pass him the fork
not true, I tell him and offer my face to the nearest ewe

when I really want to say I've been on the inside
matched them breath for breath

when I really want to tell him how I long to wrap
myself in the steaming crimson skirt she trails behind
let her lick me to my feet, push me guide me to her teat
fill me sticky sweet with life

*

the lambs started to come only two weeks ago
already I hear bleats in my head
in my still house, my quiet bed
dream amber eyes and woolly breath
and silver chords that fasten lambs to both worlds
one giving way to the other

Acknowledgements

The author would like to thank the Saskatchewan Arts Board for their financial assistance. Heartfelt thanks to my writers' group for their fine suggestions, keen perceptions, and endless topics of conversation. I am deeply grateful. Thanks to my family and my dear friends for their support, patience, and encouragement. And finally a thanks to Liz Philips for teaching.

Jeanne Marie de Moissac is a prolific poet and short fiction writer. Her works have appeared in *Grain, Dandelion, Arc, Fiddlehead,* and even *Playgirl.* She has had her work broadcast on CBC Radio.

Jeanne Marie was born and raised near Biggar, Saskatchewan, and currently lives on a farm in the Bear Hills near that town. For three years a member of the poetry circle led by Anne Szumigalski in Saskatoon, Jeanne Marie has also studied at the University of Saskatchewan.

THE OPEN EYE POETRY SERIES:

Poetry that knows where you live!

Check out the rest of the titles in the 1998 Open Eye series:

My Flesh the Sound of Rain
Heather MacLeod

A masterpiece of native and white myth and icon – an Indian shaman shares attention with the Christian Virgin and the pagan holy days Beltane and Samhain.

Sex, Death and Naked Men
Bernice Friesen

Sex, death, religion – the big questions, taken in sassy, ribald, in-your-face broadsides, or tender, tentative, thoughtful lyrics.

a slow dance in the flames
Lynda Monahan

Deeply in love with language – celebrates the perfection of nature as well as the imperfect, painful, but often alluring state of being human.

COTEAU BOOKS